THE OTHER
WOODS

George Woods

Copyright © Year 2025.

All Rights Reserved by **George Woods.**

No part of this publication may be reproduced in any form, or by any means, electronic or mechanical, including photocopying, recording, or any information browsing, storage, or retrieval system, without permission in writing from George Woods.

ISBN

Hardcover: 978-1-969844-73-7

Paperback: 978-1-969844-72-0

I. George Woods as a child

About the Author

This book is truly a gift from God. I could never have imagined writing it on my own. It was placed in my spirit with a purpose. God showed me that there would be people who might never pick up a Bible, but they would read this book and encounter His truth through it.

My journey has been anything but ordinary. I grew up in a blended family. My father had three children, and my mother had four. As a child, I was spoiled, but everything changed when my parents divorced when I was fourteen. Suddenly, the comfort was gone, and I found myself lying about my age just to get a job washing dishes. Looking back now, I realize that experience was one of the best things that could have happened to me.

At the same time, I fell into the grip of drugs, alcohol, and smoking from the age of fourteen until twenty-one. But God stepped in. He filled me with His Holy Spirit, and I was set free. By His grace, I have been clean and sober for over 47 years.

My experiences on the PGA Tour, even crossing paths with Tiger Woods, opened doors I never expected and taught me lessons I now share in these pages. I thank God for allowing me to write this book. It is more than a story. It is a reminder that God's power can transform any life.

Table of Contents

About the Author ii
My Personal Testimony 1
The Driving Range 3
The Boone Valley Golf Experience 6
The RV Revolution on Tour 11
Caddying for Craig Perks at Sawgrass 14
Ministering on Tour 17
How I Got Hooked On Drugs and Alcohol 19
Delivered by the Grace Original Text 23
The Yardage Game 29
Keep God First 34
Are You In Or You Out 38

My Personal Testimony

This sweet baby in the picture grew up to battle addiction, alcoholism, causing my mother deep worry and heartache along the way.

At the age of 14, the first alcoholic beverage I consumed was 100% Kentucky bourbon. My friends brought me home drunk, rang the doorbell, and left me in front of the door. My mother, the strong woman that she was, had to care for her doped-up, drunk child. I went down a dark path, and I hurt everyone going down it. Most of all, my mother.

My struggle went on for a while, and during this battle, my mother passed away. That made things even worse for me. I was getting high and drunk daily. This one time, during one of my worst trips, I was drunk and high, driving back, I could've sworn I felt my mother's presence in the car. I could feel her asking me, "Why are you doing this, baby?"

I knew my mom had died and gone to heaven, and if I wanted to see my mom again, I knew I had to have a radical change of life. I'm happy to say to you, it has been 47 years, and God has totally cleaned me up I have not even smoked a cigarette in 47 years when I first started smoking marijuana I relapsed after about a week and smoked half a joint but at that time I had the Holy Spirit in me and it felt like my whole world was coming apart. I prayed and I cried and I fasted for a week and a half till God finally let me know that he had forgiven me for smoking that half a joint and that I have been drug free now for 47 years, and that is the power of God.

I just want to let anybody know that if you're struggling with any kind of addiction today, just ask God to clean you up, ask God to forgive you, and he will do it; it's just that simple. As long as you try to do it yourself and make promises to yourself without meaning them from the heart, it will never happen. But when you ask God to help clean you up and help you to stop doing whatever that bad habit is, he will give you His Holy Spirit, which is your keeping power, and it will help you stop doing whatever it is that's not pleasing to yourself or to God. I hope you enjoyed the balance of my book. I wanted to share my personal testimony with you so that you'll know God is real, and how I know He's real because He lives inside of me and takes care of me every day.

He's done things for me that nobody else could do and I give him all the credit because you know when it's your will or when it's God's will and God has blessed me and brought me from so many dangerous situations and brought me to the point to write this book to share to those that might be struggling themselves, I hope you enjoyed this book thank you.

The Driving Range

I was the baby of a big, blended family. My mom, Louise Woods, had three kids when she married my dad, Sylvester Woods, who had four of his own. So, when they got married, I was the youngest of seven children. And boy, was I spoiled!

As a child, I never had to do anything for myself. If there was something I had my eye on, my parents made sure I got it. My brothers and sisters waited on me hand and foot— cleaning my room, doing chores around the house, and even giving me baths. I never had to lift a finger.

Looking back, I'm sure they resented having to cater to my every whim, but at the time, I was living the dream. We weren't a wealthy family by any means. Both my mom and dad worked hard, but they made sure I grew up in a loving, comfortable home. To me, we were rich; I had everything a kid could want— toys, clothes, you name it. Christmas was especially magical, with piles of gifts just for me. This fairytale life lasted until I was 14 years old. That's when my parents got divorced, and my world turned upside down.

It felt like I had to grow up almost overnight. I started working as a dishwasher with my brother Calvin at a restaurant called Walter Mitty's in Clayton, MO. My mom even lied about my age so I could start working at 14, two years earlier than the law allowed. It was a huge adjustment, going from living a carefree, privileged childhood to working in a restaurant. But I'm grateful to my brother Calvin for not only giving me a job, but also introducing me to golf.

The first time I visited a course, I thought I'd be a natural, just swinging away. Boy, was I wrong! I'll never forget my first time at the driving range, a 6-foot-tall, 280-pound 30-year-old trying to hit a golf ball. I duffed shot after shot, barely getting the ball off the tee. Everyone was watching, and I was so embarrassed. While I never did become the cook I dreamed of, I did get to see some of my friends work their way up to that position at the restaurant. And I found my true calling in golf, thanks to Calvin. The transition from spoiled kid to working teenager was tough, but I believe it built character. I wouldn't trade those experiences for anything.

I'm writing this book in honor of my big brother, Calvin Woods, and his beautiful wife, May. Calvin taught me a great deal about life and being a man. As a teenager, he introduced me to the game of golf, which has brought me so many amazing experiences. I wouldn't be where I am today without him.

Sadly, Calvin passed away at the age of 65, but I'll always be grateful for the time we had together. I'm 65 years old now, and I recently had a triple bypass surgery that was touch-and-go. It made me realize how precious life is and how we need to make the most of the time we have. That's why I want to share my story and my faith in Jesus Christ, my Lord and Savior. He's the reason I'm still here. Growing up, we didn't go to church regularly, but we believed in God. As I got older, after my mom passed away, I started drinking more and doing drugs. Looking back, this was a cry for help. I felt like I was in free-fall, and there was no end in sight to the pain. I was headed down a dark path.

But 44 years ago, I had a born-again experience, and God has been keeping me ever since. I started going to church more, hoping to see my mom again in heaven. I'm proud to say that I haven't touched drugs or alcohol in 44 years. God's Holy Spirit has given me the strength to stay clean and sober. I've been married to my beautiful wife Bertha, whom we call Big Bertha, for 44 wonderful years.

Every day, we wake up not knowing what challenges we'll face. But with God in my life, I know he is my keeper. He gives me the power to get through anything. When I'm weak, he is strong. There have been times when I knew I couldn't have stayed clean on my own for more than 30 days, but God has kept me going for 44 years. That's not my doing; that's the power of God at work. We all face trials in life, but we have to remember that God is on our side. God said He's more than the whole world against you. I'm so grateful for the opportunity to write this book and share my experiences, including my time on the Professional Golfers' Association of America (PGA) Tour with Tiger Woods. I know it's all a gift from God. I hope my story will inspire others to put their faith in Jesus and let him be the keeper of their lives, too.

To my brother, Calvin Woods (*10.07.1949—02.23.2015) and his loving wife, May Woods.*

The Boone Valley Golf Experience

I remember an old man that I worked with back in 1983 who was a big golfer. At the time, I thought it was one of the most boring games ever. In 1989, I went to visit my brother Calvin in Chicago, IL, and he took me to a driving range. Remember, I'm a 6-foot-tall, 280-pound 30-year-old black man, and it seemed as if everyone there was watching me to see how far this big fellow would hit the ball. This was my first golf swing ever, and what happened? I missed the whole ball. I was embarrassed but kept trying. When I did hit the ball, it went about 10 feet, and the bug bit me. That was the moment my passion for the sport was born.

One month after my embarrassing first miss, my brother Calvin came to St. Louis to play a 9-hole round with me at a public golf course in St. Louis, MO called Forest Park Golf Course. It's about 7:00 am and the tee box is full of people. My brother gets up and hits a long one down the middle of the fairway. I get up, swing, and miss. I swing again and miss the ball again. After about 5 misses, my brother walks off and yells, "Just throw the f-ing ball,". Well, I finally hit the ball and ended up having a fun day on the course with my brother.

In my quest to learn the game, I was very blessed to meet an old man named Leo. He was a regular at a little public golf course in University City, MO, called Ruth Park Golf Course, and would teach me for free. We would buy old balls and use a shag bag.

A shag bag is a bag with a tube that allows you to pick up and collect your balls after you hit them. This will save a ton of money instead of going to the driving range. I would think that there is a Leo in every city on many golf courses who loves to help others learn the game for free. I'll always be indebted to him for teaching me the game.

Once I started learning, I would play golf seven days a week. When I made my first par, it was like a new high. For those of you who may be new to the game, par is the number of strokes a player is required to complete an individual hole or all the holes on a golf course. I had made my very first par and I was hooked.

I must warn you: golf is like a powerful drug. The more you learn and do, the more you want to learn and do. It seems never to be enough. The desire is never satiated. Once bitten by the golf bug, you tend to eat, sleep, and think golf. You feel like you must find a place to go to hit the ball, even to the extent of neglecting essential things in life.

Given the addictive nature of the game, it can be easily idolized and put on a pedestal. It begins to take over your life. About golf being a metaphor for life, it can be likened to a drug, alcohol, sex, or gambling addiction that can overtake you and disrupt your life if you allow it to. You must have a godly, disciplined, and balanced mentality about it.

According to Matthew 6:33, the Kingdom of God is the thing that should be sought after, and He adds things, like golf, to your life in proper perspective. 1 Timothy 6:17 says that God gives us all things to enjoy. However, the Ten Commandments warn against idols.

Allowing the game to become front and center in your mind creates an idol out of it. It is just as self-destructive as any other addictive habit that all of a sudden you can't seem to do without. "You shall have no other gods before or besides Me. You shall not make yourself any graven image [to worship it] or any likeness of anything that is in the heavens above, or that is in the earth beneath, or that is in the water under the earth...." Exodus 20:3-4 (Amplified version).

When I first started playing the game, I was accused of spending too much time playing golf. I couldn't see how I was putting it before God, but my wife and even my pastor were on my case about the amount of time I was spending on golf. I took a look at what they were saying, realized they were right, and put the game in its proper perspective.

1 Corinthians 14:40 states, "Let all things be done decently and in order." Golf is one of those "things" that must be kept in order. It took the power of God through Jesus Christ to help me break the hold that the love for the game had on me.

So, let's talk about how I got the job on the PGA tour. It all started with playing golf at Ruth Park golf course. One day, some guys pulled up late in the afternoon, and I was a marshal. The marshal is the guy who rides around the course and makes sure the flow of play is going well. One of the guys asked me if I would run back to the clubhouse and get him a six-pack of beer, which is something I normally don't do. However, I went ahead and got him a pack of beer and when I came back out, he asked me if I would be interested in coming out to host the caddie tent at the Boone Valley Classic, which was the Senior PGA Tour event, they were having at Boone Valley Golf Club located in Augusta, MO in 1996. I told him I would be happy to come out and try it out.

My wife and I had to go through a Federal Bureau of Investigation (FBI) background check, and it turned out to be a blessing for us. The first year that I went out, I used to own a pallet business (wooden pallets), and we would grind up all of our old wood waste, and so the tournament ended up buying 8 tractor-trailer loads of wood chips from me. So, I would go out to Boone Valley every year and pick up a check for about $8,000 and eat well all week and be around pro golfers, which I love, and get to know all the caddies and their friends. Lee Trevino's caddie gave me his caddie bib, and I donated it to the golf course. I got to know all the caddies, and they got to know me.

The guy who got me the job at Boone Valley was Brian Manziel. The young man was the head chef out there which meant ate good. We had breakfast and lunch, and all the food was top-of-the-line. It was such an enjoyable time watching these guys play golf, getting to know them, and going fishing on the property. I met the caddie for David Graham, his name is Steve Hulka, and we became brothers in Christ. He wrote the PGA tour for me and got me my own credential as the full-time caddie chaplain.

I went out on tour with Steve Hulka to a tournament at Torrey Pines Golf Course in 2000. At that time, Tiger Woods had won six in a row. I flew from St. Louis to San Diego, CA. Steve Hulka had the PGA tour transportation pick me up at the airport. They pulled up in a Buick that had the tournament name on both sides of the doors and two big white posters in the back windows that said Woods.

The people were gathering around the car, and when I stepped outside, I could read the confusion on their faces. They probably thought *This guy is too fat to be Tiger. Who is this guy? Is he, his dad?* (They must have thought I was related because my last name is Woods, and the players, along with some of their families, were given courtesy cars for the tournament.)

This 70-year-old volunteer took my clubs and put them in the trunk of the car, and he said, 'Should I take you to pick up your courtesy car now, Mr. Woods?' I said Man, you need to take me straight to the course.

You must remember that at a PGA Tour Tournament, there are only a handful of people of color at each tournament. You only had a few players on the PGA Tour of color. Vijay Singh, and only a couple more people who were of color, and very few caddies who were of color, that would have a PGA Tour credential or badge around their neck, and I was one of those few.

A lot of people thought I might have been Earl Woods or a distant relative of Tiger's that they had never seen. It was so funny to me what people would ask me, different things at different tournaments about do I know Tiger, am I his dad, or maybe his cousin, I would get it from every angle. I would be walking in a crowd of people, and we would all be watching the golf tournament, and then two or three of them would just start whispering right behind me, and they would just whisper, and then they finally asked me, "Are you related to Tiger?" Of course, I would tell them I wasn't but that they could pretend I was if it made their day better.

A lot of people would ask me for autographs, which I never declined. At the time, I thought it was hilarious. I don't know how many people today have a signed autograph by "George Woods," thinking they got some kind of relic of Tiger Woods. Maybe when this book comes out, they will have a laugh just like I did at that time, and they will have something to hold onto.

Then September 11, 2001, happened, and of course, everything changed. Steve began an over-the-road business to take the players' clubs from tournament to tournament. He bought a truck and a trailer, and

Steve and I would take all their extra luggage and transport it to the next tournament so they could get on the plane with just their briefcases.

He called it Hulka Over the Road Express. Steve and I would drive the truck non-stop to the next tournament and sometimes we had to travel 800 miles. However, sometimes we didn't have to travel more than 300 miles, but we would get there as quickly as possible because we had all the players' clubs. Steve Hulka was a caddie for Chip Beck at the time. We would get to the tournament, and he would go on caddie duty; I would take all the players' luggage and put it in their lockers or be at the truck until they came and picked up their luggage.

One of the best parts of working in this over-the-road business is getting well acquainted with some of my favorite golfers. I didn't know it at the time, but this was yet another door God had opened for me.

It takes all types to make the world, and while most of these pro golfers were extremely polite, there were a few who were less pleasant to be around. I won't be mentioning them in this book. Steve is still providing the service today, and his son Ben has also become a caddie. I'm extremely proud of the success they've seen on the PGA Tour. Steve Hulka is an old-school caddie; all the players used to carry their watches and extra change in a Crown Royal Velvet bag. Steve reminds me of that Crown Royal Velvet bag. Steve is a good Christian brother and has a concern about the souls that are out on the PGA tour. Steve would come and stay with my wife, Bertha, and me as we got to know Steve year after year. This went on for about three years, and Steve would stay at our house, and we would have a wonderful time, play golf, go fishing, and just do fun things.

The RV Revolution on Tour

There was a bus explosion on the PGA tour, where everybody started buying RV buses to travel. When I first came out on the PGA tour, two people had buses, which were John Daly and Davis Love III. We went from two buses out on tour to about twelve buses out on tour, it seemed like within 30 days. Most players would buy a $500,000 to $600,000 bus called a Holiday Rambler. The buses had all the luxuries of what you would have at home, plus all the privacy for the player and his family, and they could travel comfortably on these buses. At one point, so many people were buying buses out there that Holiday Rambler would have a repairman travel with the tour just so that they could maintain and fix the buses.

It became a little town within itself, and the PGA Tour would arrange for all these buses to park somewhere near or on the course. Since these buses were always on the go, I had the bright idea to start pressure washing them. I ended up making some really good money. Then some of the players found out that I had a CDL license, meaning that I could drive a tractor-trailer, so they started hiring me to transport their buses from tournament to tournament.

I remember one time I was driving Davis Love III's bus, and he had about a $2M bus, one of the most expensive buses out there. Almost all of the buses had a CB radio in them, but they looked like they didn't have one. I enjoyed listening to the truck drivers talking over the CB radios. I could overhear their bewilderment at seeing a black man driving this expensive bus. There must've been a handful of colored people driving around that bus in the US.

I would imagine that when people would see a young black man driving a two-million-dollar bus and pull up at a fuel station to get fuel, they were just thinking that I was some sort of rapper.

I did try to look for more black people driving such buses, but in vain…Actually, I take that back— there was one black couple that I ran into who had a Holiday Rambler. It was a nice bus and we made small talk, but I never saw anybody else out there who was of color.

Once, an old lady at a gas station came up to me and asked if the bus was mine. I almost told her it was my third one, but I didn't want to lie. I just said I was transporting it for someone else from Florida to California. But it was a sweet gig, I got paid well, ate good food, and flew back home to St. Louis.

Lee Janzen was one of the professional golfers out there at the time, and he and I would talk, and he would ask me different questions about driving the buses. He asked me how I came up with the idea of driving the buses and power washing them when I got to each tournament. I told him, "Mr. Needmore and I had a talk, and he thought it was a good idea." Lee said, "Who is Mr. Needmore?" I told him, "Mr. Need-More Money!"

I tell you, driving the buses and washing the buses became a full-time job for me. One time, I was moving Lee Janzen's van, and he had his dog in there with me. We stopped for gas and somehow the dog got out and ran right in front of an 18-wheeler!

I had to risk my life chasing after that little dog. Nearly cost us our lives! Scariest moment of my life! I didn't tell Janzen what happened at first. But eventually Steve Hulka, whom I was close with, let it slip. Janzen didn't say anything until I got to the course. He just looked at me and said, "So, you got a story for me about my dog?" I was so relieved that the dog made it!

I hired a friend of mine, Nate Wilson, who would help me drive these buses each week, and it was so much fun. I said one day I was going to buy myself one, and maybe after I get through writing this book, I may be able to afford one with the help of the good Lord.

I remember one time we ate at a Chinese restaurant after Jack Nicklaus's tournament in Ohio. I was not thinking when I went in to book the reservation, but I booked it under my last name, Woods, and it was about eight caddies that all went out to eat dinner. We got in the restaurant and went to the buffet line to get our food. A Chinese woman came up to me and said she had a question she wanted to ask me. I said, "Sure." And she asked, "Are you Tiger Woods' father?". It took me all my strength to look her in the face and say, "I might just have a little Earl in me."

The bus driving job lasted about two years, and then suddenly things started changing. Their kids got older, and the expense of maintaining the buses became impractical, and people started selling their buses off.

It still amazes me how God takes care of me and has allowed me to start my own little business, where I make a pretty good income each week cleaning buses and transporting them from event to event.

Caddying for Craig Perks at Sawgrass

My first experience caddying on the PGA Tour came in dramatic fashion in March of 2003. I was at TPC Sawgrass, headquarters of the PGA Tour, helping Steve Hulka drive from tournament to tournament. I would usually get up every morning about five, have breakfast, and head down to the caddie area.

Steve would go do a shift, and I would just sit around. Sometimes, I'd discuss religion and the Bible with some of the other guys or see if they would want me to do anything for them. I had a very close relationship with Andrew Martinez, Tom Lehman's caddie. One morning I was in the caddie area when the Caddie Master came in looking for a substitute—you see, one of the guys had gotten arrested the night before. Andrew turned to him and said, "I've got just the guy— take Big George!" I really had no idea who he was talking about until the Master came over to me and asked me for help. Of course, I told him yes. I didn't know who I was carrying for or where I was going. I followed him out to the driving range, and then he took me to Craig Perks, who was leading the tournament from the night before.

Excitedly, I introduced myself to Mr. Perks. I assured him that I'm here if he needs anything at all. He just gave me a knowing look and told me he just needed me to carry his bag and keep up with him. He said when he stops, he wants his bag right next to him since he liked to lean on it and clean his shoes before every shot. I understood and told him my golden rule of caddying: *Keep up, and shut up.*

So, we were paired up with Davis Love III and Vijay Singh. We went out to the last shot they hit before dark the night before, and we were halfway out in the fairway on the 15th hole, so we played to the 15th hole. Vijay Singh and Davis Love III parred the hole from the night before, and Craig Perks birdied the hole from the night before. Then we got to hole number 16 (par-5) and Mr. Perks striped another one right down the middle. He hit a great second shot and positioned himself to get on the green in three.

He got a nice third shot put about ten feet away from the flag, and we made a birdie, another birdie, we are now two under par. We come to hole number 17, the famous island green. Craig Perks hit 1 in there about 2 feet under the cup. Davis Love III hit a shot that went wide on the green, but it stayed on the green. Vijay Singh hit his shot into the water. Craig Perks tapped in his third birdie on the famous island green, Davis Love III made his par of course, and Vijay Singh made a bogey. After that hole was over, Davis Love III walked up to me and said, "Dude, you're a super caddy!"

So, we got to hole 18 and Craig Perks hit one immediately. Vijay Singh piped one right down the middle, and Davis Love III hit a great shot down the middle. My guy Craig Perks punched his ball out into the middle of the fairway and accidentally hit Vijay Singh's ball. The three players came together to determine where Vijay's ball had originally been lying. Vijay was already frustrated and standing over his shot, ready to hit, when suddenly the cameraman on the course shouted, "Don't hit that! That's not where your ball was!"

I've never seen a Brown man turn red before, but Vijay was furious. Meanwhile, Craig stepped up, stuck his next shot in there nice and tight, and walked off with a par.

Now I come in from the 18th hole, and I had news reporters everywhere asking me questions about caddying for Craig Perks. Davis Love III won the tournament and came to me after he had won and said that if I had stayed on Craig Perk's bag, he would have lost by three strokes. After I had finished with the media, I went back to the caddie area where the rest of the caddies were. The other caddies immediately dubbed me "TOW— The Other Woods." A play on my last name and Tiger. I couldn't help but laugh, feeling God's sense of humor at work.

The caddies back then had some great nicknames. There was "Jelly", a big guy who looked like a jelly roll. "Rabbit" was a skinny dude who resembled a rabbit or squirrel. "Swifty" was the smooth operator.

Caddying for Craig Perks at the Players was an unforgettable experience. I was just trying to keep up, but Perks played great golf. It was an honor to carry his bag, even for just one round. And the way the other players and caddies embraced me made it even more special. I knew God had orchestrated the whole thing. It was a day I'll never forget, and a reminder that with faith, anything is possible.

Ministering on Tour

I started holding Bible classes on Tuesday nights during tours. I felt gratified in teaching the other caddies about the word of God. There was another Bible study group on Wednesdays that I would attend.

Initially, I didn't have a great turnout because when most caddies got off, they were going to get something to eat or to drink, or going back to their hotel room. I had four or five that were faithful and would come every time. I remember we had a player come to one of my Bible studies one time— Aaron Baddeley. I was elated to see how learned he was. An extremely spiritual man.

Since most caddies would not come out to the Bible study, I decided that I would just print the teachings out on what I called the Good News Journal and pass them out every week. I would do different lesson topics, typing out three or four paragraphs on each. I got a better response thanks to this journal. There were still some people who'd see me coming with my pile of journals and run the other way. But more often than not, people would see me and say, "Hey, where'd my journal at?"

I would do a lot of one-on-ones with caddies. I would talk to them about where my believe stemmed from. I would share stories of my darkest hour— the years I struggled with alcohol and drugs. I would tell them about how God delivered me from these vices, and I had been clean for so many years and that I knew it was the power of God because I couldn't have lasted that long.

At the time of writing this book, I have been drug and alcohol free for over 44 years. This is a shock to anyone who knew me back then— I wouldn't have lasted one month. I have not taken a drink of alcohol or done drugs in 44 years. Not a day goes by when I don't thank Jesus for giving me the strength to fight my demons.

To be able to engage with the others, I tried to discuss hot topics which I knew would resonate with them. I would talk about drinking, gambling, and how to be a better Christian. I would also explain to them how the Holy Spirit works. I would explain that it was God's keeping power that kept us all the time, not ourselves. As you read on, you'll find out about things that I used to do, which I don't anymore. No desire to hang out with your old drug addict and alcoholic friends, all you want to do is praise God and go to church and worship him for delivering you from that reckless life.

Amazing Grace, how sweet the sound,
That saved a wretch like me!
I once was lost, but now am found.
— Amazing Grace, Hayley Westenra

These lyrics really ring true. The beautiful thing about serving God is that when a positive change happens in your life, you know it's a result of your personal relationship with God. There will be things that have happened in every believer's life that only God can change and that only God can do. He builds that relationship with a believer, and nobody is exempt from a relationship with God.

I suggest deep reflection if you don't have a relationship with God, or if you don't turn to Him in tough times, or in happy days. Because without Him we can do nothing; we cannot even breathe the air entering our lungs without the power of God. God will set us up in life, so that when things come to pass, we know that it is Him and not ourselves. I could not have thought of getting a job out on the PGA Tour doing Bible studies with the caddies; it was the power of God that gave me that job. I believe God put me out there when Tiger was dominating the tournaments, and my last name was Woods.

How I Got Hooked On Drugs and Alcohol

As I stated earlier in the book, I grew up in a beautiful home with two loving parents. But no relationship is without hardships. My parents would fight quite often, and I would see things that a child should never see. At the age of fourteen, my father left the house. It's left us kids without a disciplinarian in the house.

I started getting out of control. As a way of coping with my parents' divorce, I started drinking alcohol at the age of fourteen. I remember the first drink that I took was 100 Proof Kentucky Bourbon. I was so drunk that when my friends took me home, I was vomiting my guts out. I was so drunk that they got me out of the car and leaned me up against my front door, rang the doorbell, and took off. My mom came to the door. I still remember the panic in her voice as she tried to figure out what had happened. I just crawled to the bathroom and started puking. Because that was the first time that I had drunk alcohol, and I was 14 years old, it broke my mother's heart to see her child in that state. Of course, we went from drinking alcohol to smoking weed and then doing hard drugs. Things just went downhill for me from there.

My best friend's name was Floyd Gaston, but everyone called him Rookie. Rookie and I were about the same age as some of his older cousins, who were really into hot rods and loved working on them. Just about every day after school, we'd walk home and see his cousins out on the street with their cars, hanging out and drinking. Because of that, I could stop and get drunk pretty much anytime I wanted during the week.

Of course, we were also smoking dope and taking pills. I remember Rookie introduced me to Purple Microdot— a form of LSD. Initially, I was hesitant. I had heard that LSD trips were dangerous. I contemplated taking the drug for the next six months. Then one day, I decided to try it while I was at school. This was a terrible decision.

Rookie told everybody that I was high on acid, so everyone thought it was a fun idea to mess with my head. I remember walking down the hallway, and somebody was standing on the second floor; they called my name. I looked up, and they dropped a single piece of paper. But to me, it looked like a thousand rocks were crashing down from the ceiling. I dropped to the floor, grabbed my head, and started screaming.

One of the teachers came by and checked up on me. They got me up off the floor. I went to industrial arts class, where we would build screwdrivers and hammerheads out of metal. We never began working with the industrial furnace without the teacher's presence in the classroom. The teacher was always two or three minutes late.

That day, I went to the back and fired up the furnace, got my hammerhead project out, and started hammering my project, watching the sparks fly off.

If any of you out there have ever done acid, you know exactly what I was seeing. If I saw one spark, it looked like a hundred—like a full-blown light show. Every time I took my hammer and hit it with another hammer, sparks would fly, and I'd just sit there watching in awe.

At one point, I ended up melting down a project I had spent nearly two months working on in metal class—completely ruined it. The teacher walked in and yelled, "George, what are you doing?!"

A friend of mine, Rolling Thornton, was in class with me. He looked at the teacher and said, "Mr. Gibson, you've got to excuse George Woods—he took a hit of acid this morning."

I freaked out. I thought for sure I was going to jail. But the teacher just looked at me, shook his head, and said, "Sit down, young man," then started laughing.

The class started, and all the guys in the class got together and decided to mess with my head. They went around and were talking to me, but they were not saying anything; they were just moving their mouths. I can hear the hammers going, I can hear the drills, but every time somebody came up and said something to me, they would just move their mouth, and they would not let words come out and I was freaking out. They freaked me out so badly in that class that I left the classroom and went to my locker to get my things out of my locker because I was planning to go home.

I could not take it anymore with such stuff going on. As I turn the lock on my locker to do the combination, I would go right, I would go left, and as I spun the locker the numbers would fly off the locker into the air and I could see the numbers flying off the locker into the air because I had taken a hit of acid and it was time for me to leave the school. I remember walking outside, and it felt like I was in a Looney Tunes episode with Bugs Bunny and those characters, and it was the weirdest feeling that I had ever had, but it was fun. When I took a hit of acid, the high would normally last around 8 to 10 hours, depending on whether I wanted to come down or not.

My brother Calvin and I gave a New Year's Eve party one time, and we made a bowl of punch and put about twenty hits of acid in it and told everybody not to drink the punch if they didn't want to freak out since it had acid in it.

People were drinking the punch just because we told them not to. That was one of the craziest, wildest parties I've ever been to in my life. Folks were dancing in ways I'd never seen before—moving wild, twisting, just completely letting loose. It was a New Year's Eve party like no other. We had to take one of my friends who had never drank alcohol or done drugs to the emergency room because he drank some of the punch, and he was feeling awful.

Acid became my drug of choice for about a year. I remember as I kept doing acid that my whole personality changed. I started wearing a blue derby hat with a scarf tied around it (like Jimi Hendrix), wearing blue jeans, and would go around most of the time with no shoes on. I had really let myself go.

It really hurt my mom to see me change so radically and in such a negative way. There was a young lady who lived on the floor below us, and she was a heroin addict. I found out that she would have her acid specially made since normal acid was not strong enough for her. Jerome Gregory, a friend of mine, had returned from the service, and we decided to drop acid together. I'm so glad I share half with my buddy. It was so potent that I know if I took it by myself, I would have been in a mental asylum because it would have fried my brain.

This realization was the reason why I stopped taking acid. So, that was one drug I decided not to take anymore. Soon after, I joined the church.

It has been 44 years since I have taken any drugs or drunk alcohol. I know in my heart that had it not been for my faith, I may have lasted 30 days. I remember starting to hang out with all my drug addict friends again, five years after I had been in church. One time, they were all sitting in a kitchen passing around some weed around the table. When the joint came to me, I refused. Most of them didn't even recognize me anymore. Not only did I recover from drug and alcohol abuse, but I looked different, too. If you do drugs on a consistent basis and drink a bunch of alcohol, it changes your structure, your life, your personality; you do not even look like the same person.

It amazes me how long God has been keeping me away from these vices. I am thankful that He has given me His Holy Spirit, strengthening my resolve. I do not even have a desire to do any alcohol or drugs— I don't feel a pull towards that life anymore. I can just think about how good God has made my life—I can get higher than any pill or any alcohol has ever made me, just thinking about His goodness and His mercy.

Delivered by the Grace Original Text

I'd like to talk about some of the great times the caddies and I used to have playing golf when we were on the road. One time when we were in California, we went to Indio Municipal Golf Course—a par-3 course. It's lit up so that you can play at night. At least fifteen guys showed up that night, including Bubba Watson's caddie, Ted Scott. I could smell marijuana all over the course, but I couldn't be certain who was smoking up.

I got up to a hole, and of course, no one was paying any attention to me, so naturally, I sank a hole-in-one. Now, you know the pastor's not supposed to be gambling, but when that ball dropped, my buddy Steve Hulka, the one who got me in the game, told everyone I was in on the bet. So just like that, I walked away with something like $400 that night. It was wild.

The very next hole, everybody was wondering what I was going to do next, and they were all teasing me and saying I couldn't do it again. So, to prove them wrong, I got on the next hole. Everybody watched me swing, and I hit a banana hook that ran up on the green and almost went in for a second ace! Everyone was cracking up, saying things like "Oh my God, he almost did it again! Only The Other Woods could pull that off!"

The next day, word had spread about my near back-to-back aces. Suddenly, I had the respect and admiration of all the caddies. They saw that I could play a little golf. But more importantly, they saw the joy and peace I had, something they were still searching for. You see, I believe God has a great sense of humor. The way he orchestrated my experiences on the PGA Tour, from my last name to the doors he opened, is a testament to his plan for my life.

I know a lot of people look at God as this strict, mean being meant to be feared, but I tell you now that God has a funny sense of humor. I traveled with the PGA tour for over 10 years and drove the players' buses and helped Steve Hulka drive over the road. My wife Bertha and I enjoyed the traveling very much. When you're traveling so often, you get used to it. Even though we were traveling for work, it never felt like work. Hopefully, after I finish this book, I will be able to go back out on the PGA Tour and write about the back nine.

I always enjoy coming back home and playing golf with my golfing friends and telling them all the wild stories and things that happened to me out on the PGA Tour. I remember playing golf with one of my golfing friends, and he says, "Hey, Woods, you talk like you are a member of the PGA Tour." I said, "Hey, man, I am." As you travel and play different courses you meet a lot of different people in every state and I've made some good relationships over the years traveling and playing golf and just telling people about God and the PGA Tour and how God opens doors in your life, he'll give you your heart's desire if you trust him.

So, here I am finally writing this book after my triple bypass surgery in 2021. God blessed me to still be on the face of this Earth. I pray that someone will read this book and understand that there are certain things in your life that only God can do. Certain doors that only God can open, and being on the PGA Tour for me was one of those doors.

I give all credit and praise to God for creating a path for me to be out on the PGA Tour, and for allowing me to write this book with the last name—Woods— which is one of the most enjoyable things I have done in my life. I do not take life for granted anymore since I have had triple bypass surgery and came within an inch of my life. I thank God for another day's journey, and his mercy and grace.

I don't know what you believe or how you believe, one thing is for sure: we all understand that we must leave this earth one day if God does not return before then. Most people don't like thinking about life after death, but it is something that we should reflect on. We should get our affairs in order in this life so when we meet our maker, we can hold our heads high. That is one thing I love about serving God— it is a personal relationship, something everyone should have with their maker.

When I was spiraling into the abyss, I came very close to losing my life. I look back and realize that it was not just me, but God had a plan for my life even when I was using drugs and alcohol, even when I wasn't the best Christian. Being delivered from drug and alcohol addiction, I was able to relate to the caddies on tour who have had addiction issues. Many of them drink and do drugs exclusively.

It's very difficult for struggling addicts to go on golf tours. There is a party most of the time, and the alcohol is free, and the drugs are easily accessible. With temptation all around, sobriety because very difficult. This is where I see the need for a ministry. It took Jesus Christ to deliver me from my sinful ways, and my alcoholism and drug addiction. A lot of people think it is all a life of glamour, as it's portrayed in the media and all that, but I am sure there are even players who struggle with addictions. There are people on tour who need deliverance from drug abuse, gambling addictions, sexual addiction, alcoholism, and a lot of other things. I see it all the time, I know the signs all too well.

I have known people who have had gambling addictions in the past. They would pick up a paper in the morning just to see what they could gamble on as if they were always looking to make the next hustle. They count their money on the road, and the only way to get more money is to take a dollar and make it into $10.

There is a need for a ministry when somebody has a gambling problem. They get depressed when they lose, and it drives them into a deeper, darker hole that they need to get out of. My job is to try and reach them, deliver them from these addictions. Someone may be thinking: *What does it mean to be delivered? How does one get delivered?*

After my parents divorced when I was fourteen, my mom had a hard time dealing with me. She battled cancer for five years, and eventually, she passed away during her illness. During that time, I was completely strung out—I drank constantly, couldn't eat, and lost a lot of weight. I was a total mess. I didn't even make it to the hospital before she died.

When she passed, my family had to come find me. They cleaned me up just so I could attend the funeral. I remember standing there, looking at her in the coffin, and I couldn't even cry. I felt so much guilt and pain that it just shut me down. I loved my mom deeply, but I was completely lost in addiction.

After the funeral, I went back home, and it hit me—there was no one there to clean up, no one to cook, no one waiting. My mom was gone. That day, I felt like a baby. Alone. Helpless. Broken.

I'm ashamed to admit that my addiction was so bad that even after her death, I would take her checkbook to get money to support my addiction. Drinking and doing drugs, having car accidents, I was on a self-destructive path. Even while my life was headed for destruction, I would feel her presence in the car with me. In my subconscious, it was as if my mom was begging me to stop.

After this, I started thinking about heaven. I know that such a God-loving woman would go to heaven, and I wanted to get there if I ever wanted to see her again. This meant that I was going to have to change my lifestyle.

This is when I started getting sickened by myself. When you get sick of yourself, change is inevitable. I moved in with my father for a little bit and would open up a Bible once in a while. But I was still drinking, smoking marijuana, and doing drugs. Then I got a job, which caused me to tighten up on the drinking and the drugs. I soon relapsed, stopped reading the Bible, and got back into my old habits, only on the weekends now. I stopped reading my Bible and would drink and do drugs on the weekend. My father noticed and confronted me. He told me that I was doing better when I was unemployed, but since I started working, I had given up on reading the Bible and getting high on the weekends.

I knelt down to pray the Lord's Prayer. At the time, the only prayer I really knew was that childhood one: *"Now I lay me down to sleep, I pray the Lord my soul to keep."* So that's what I prayed.

After I finished, I heard a small, quiet voice say to me, "Promise me you'll quit smoking cigarettes."

It hit me hard—my dad had just been diagnosed with blood clots in his legs. The doctors warned him that if he didn't stop smoking, he could lose both legs or even suffer a massive heart attack. So when I got up off my knees, I made a commitment right then and there: I wouldn't smoke another cigarette.

And the next morning, I didn't. But I did smoke some marijuana.

A couple of weeks later, on a Thursday night—right before payday, when I was getting ready to buy my weekend supply of weed and beer—I heard that same soft voice again: "Promise me you'll stop smoking marijuana and drinking."

But right after that, another voice spoke up in my head: "George, you know you can't keep that promise."

Those voices started going back and forth inside me, like a battle—one calling me higher, the other pulling me back.

I made up my resolve. I promised myself to quit. I got up, fell on the bed, and cried like a baby. It felt like a weight was lifted off me. The next day, my dad picked me up from work. I was around 22 years old at the time, and my dad knew that I smoked weed and drank every weekend.

So, he asked me if I needed to go to the liquor store, but I refused. I went home and took a shower. Before I went to the bathroom, a friend of mine showed up with weed and alcohol. I told him I was detoxing and that I wouldn't be joining him from now on.

Soon after I cleaned up my act, God sent me my wife. Instead of going out to hang out with my drug buddies and drinking buddies, I would go with her and her mom and read the Bible. Even though I didn't share in their passion for Bible-reading, they were cooking plenty of good soul food, and it had me eating like it was Sunday morning every day. Do you see I had a total turnaround?

At this time, God had given me his spirit. I did not know it because I did not know the word of God. But something had happened to me. God delivered me, and I did not even want any more drugs or alcohol or cigarettes.

Every person knows their own limitations, and during that time in my life, I could not even go more than 30 days without some type of drug or alcohol in my system. Now that I am finally writing this book, it has been 44 years since I confessed to God with my mouth that I would not do any more drugs and alcohol, and I believed in my heart as I made these promises. I had promised God I would stop doing drugs and drinking after making this promise, and I smoked half of a joint.

The Holy Spirit was living in me now, and I had become a new creature in Christ. I slipped up and smoked a half a joint, and it felt like my whole world was coming to an end because I had made this promise to God that meant more to me than anything. I slipped up and smoked half a joint and felt like my whole world was coming down on me, and I just wanted to die.

You would've thought someone had died by my reaction to this—but deep down, I knew He had forgiven me. And I needed that moment of Godly sorrow, because it led me to true repentance. That's what finally brought me to the point where I never touched drugs again.

The Yardage Game

I'd like to mention some funny stories from my time with the other caddies and players. Teddy, who was a rookie caddie for Bubba Watson at the time, was once asked how far it was to carry a bunker. He casually said, "About a 2-iron." Bubba asked again, "No, how far is it to carry the bunker?" Teddy replied, "About 250 yards."

Then Bubba said, "Take out your yardage book."

Teddy paused and said, "Yardage book? I thought you had the book!"

It was hilarious, especially considering all the success they've had together since then, with multiple wins and great tournaments. Just shows how far they've come.

I remember sitting in the caddie area where they would serve food, and I remember that Tiger Woods was losing one of the major tournaments. All the players in there that were hating on Tiger and talking about how he deserved to lose, and that he's doing this and he's doing that. Then the N-word echoes through the room. Someone had blurted it out, forgetting that I was in the room. The room went silent and then someone said, "Watch your mouth, George is sitting here."

It is not enough just to be a caddie on the PGA Tour; you must build relationships with your players. Caddies and players have a father-son relationship, some caddies and players have a friend-friend relationship, and there are different types of relationships out on tour. One of the toughest challenges as a caddie is keeping your player both playing well and staying happy. You're constantly juggling his personal life and professional game, trying to find the balance that keeps everything on track.

Caddying is way more than just carrying a bag for a player. You must make that player feel that you have confidence in what you are doing and that you helped him to get that ball in that hole as quickly as possible.

I have caddied for a few tournaments, but most of them have been tournaments that were Pro-Am tournaments, and I can tell you amateurs want to feel like they know what they are doing. Caddying is not for everyone because if you give a player a bad yardage and he hits a bad shot, you are the blame for that, and if he hits a bad shot and you give them the right yardage, you are still to blame for that.

I remember one time I was asked to caddie for Lee Janzen at the John Deere Classic. I wore my golf shoes with spikes on them, and they were making marks all over the green. At about the fourth hole, Lee Janzen finally asks me if I have spikes on my shoes. But since I was on the golf course, I was supposed to wear my golf shoes since I was carrying, and I was just making spike marks everywhere on the greens and the player Lee looked at me and said "Hey dude, go get some tennis shoes and get those spikes off the course." It was hilarious to me because I should have known better, but I did not, and we almost made the cut. I think we missed the cut by one shot.

The players would also have a bible study on Tuesday nights. The bible studies would attract most of the Christian guys who really had a strong belief in Christ. Aaron Baddeley comes to mind as one of the youngest guys out on tour who really has a strong walk with Christ.

But then, of course, you had guys like Lee Janzen, Ben Crane, Stewart Cink, and many others. It's not easy being a player and a Christian on the PGA Tour. There's temptation everywhere—women chasing after your money, alcohol, drugs, and the kind of lifestyle that can pull you in fast.

It truly takes the power of the Holy Spirit to keep walking that narrow path—to stay faithful to your wife, your children, and to God. It's only by God's grace that we're able to stand strong. Without the Holy Spirit guiding you, temptation can quickly take over, and before you know it, you're right back in the world of sin.

At this time that I am writing this book, I have had triple bypass surgery and a stroke, and it slowed me down from writing and I'm just now picking back up where I left off. It is so funny because the stroke affected how I think. I'm not good with numbers, addresses, or credit card numbers anymore. I could not even activate a credit card. However, most people tell me how great I look; they actually say I physically look better now than I did before I had the stroke, and that is so weirdly funny to me.

I know that God has a sense of humor because there are so many things that he has allowed me to do. I thank God for having a sense of humor because I know that God put me in this position so I can finish this book and hopefully help someone else from going down a dark path.

I thank God for giving me another chance to finish this book after my stroke. It's truly a blessing to be able to tell my story. I know for a fact that God told me there would be people who read this book—*The Other Woods*—who might never pick up a Bible. And if you're one of those people, I want you to know this: *God is real.*

If you ask me, how do I know that God is real, all I need to do is look back on my own life and look at what he has done for me personally. When I was addicted to drugs and alcohol and was on my way out of here, God delivered me from my vices,

Now that I know the word of God and see all the things that Christ did for me, not only me but for everyone that I know, without a shadow of doubt that God lives in my soul, and giving me the knowledge and courage to write this book to hopefully help someone else understand how real God is.

For me to get a job out on the PGA Tour with the last name Woods is an act of God to me. The world knows who Tiger Woods is, but nobody knows who George Woods is.

Tiger Woods has millions, and probably billions, of dollars; he has all the money you'll ever need, while I'm sitting here as I write this book, homeless. My wife and I are living with my son because we got caught in between rent when I got sick, and I couldn't pay my rent for four months due to my massive heart attack.

Still, I thank God for the Holy Ghost and my children who have helped us out. The Bible tells us to help those who are less fortunate, and there's always somebody in need of help. I thank God for my wife,

Bertha. I do not know how she has put up with me for 44 years, but she has.

What I love about God is that he has a personal relationship with each human being that he desires and brings them into his kingdom; he loves all of us. I am here to tell you that when God touches your life, that is a beautiful thing. I have never seen God, but I can feel his presence. You want to know how I know God is there? It's because there are things that I cannot do that he has done for me. The only thing that I would advise for anyone who doesn't believe my testimony is to try God for yourself if you're struggling with something in your life. It could be drug, alcohol, sex, or gambling addiction, anything that you can't seem to control. Invite God in and ask for His help to let go of the things you're struggling with. Trust that He loves you so deeply, He'll make it personal—He'll meet you right where you are and help you overcome whatever feels out of your control. And in that process, you'll come to know for yourself just how real God truly is.

Nothing, no amount of fame or wealth, compares with your relationship with Christ. That is Eternal. In this life, we're lucky if we live to be 75 – 80 years old; we hardly make it to 100 anymore. But life with Him is eternal, and it's what we should strive for. That's why I'm writing this book to share with you all how important it is to have your personal relationship with God. This is a story about a member of the PGA Tour, traveling from place to place every week and golfing every Sunday. Every weekend, they must play. God is still a part of their life—they even hold a church service in the middle of the week.

But I want to say to you, there is nothing like a good Sunday morning service with pious people in a church praising and thanking God for all he has done for them that week. Without church, we wouldn't have the strength we do. As you keep reading this book, and if you're going through any kind of situation in your life, I want you to pause for a moment. Stop and ask God to help you with whatever it is you're facing. I promise you, if you ask from your heart, God will step in. He'll help you with that problem in a way so clear, so personal, that when it's resolved, you'll know without a doubt—it was God. He is real.

We become so caught up in this life, trying to make a living and keep up in the rat race, that we forget about God. Not to forget that all of us will have to leave this earth one day, that this world is not our home, and we should not plan on being down here for long periods of time. It's only God who is interested in how we can make our lives better through Christ Jesus. I thank God for the PGA Tour, which has treated me well, and I thank God for giving me an opportunity to hang out, and now I'm recovering from my heart surgery, and I have to really work hard on my golf swing to get back my energy and the strength that I had in my muscles.

Having an operation has affected every part of my body—something most people don't really understand. Even though it was a triple bypass surgery, it impacted my legs, my arms, and even my brain. I'm still struggling, trying to come back to where I once was—or better, if that's God's will. That's my goal. And I truly thank God for every prayer that was said for me while I was sick. Those prayers have meant everything.

My goal is to return to the PGA Tour and reconnect with some of my golf buddies and former players who have supported me over the years. I just thank God for another chance. I don't know what some of you may be going through in life while reading this book, but please understand that we all get a second chance if we recognize what God is capable of. In fact, look at what has happened in your life until now and know that God gave you a second chance, so I thank God for being such a kind God friendly God, and caring God, thank God for his son Jesus Christ who died on that cross for the whole world, thank God for giving us a second chance.

Keep God First

Today's date is 05/27/2022, and you won't believe it—I'm going back to work. I was hired today in transportation, and I'm so happy. Years ago, I learned how to drive a tractor-trailer, and now I get to do it again. Back when I had my pallet business, Schnucks Supermarket was one of my biggest customers, and I had over thirty people working for me. I've passed all the tests, passed my DOT physical, and I'm officially going back to driving a tractor-trailer. I love to drive, and I thank God for another opportunity to support my wife, support my family, and put food on the table.

Hopefully, by the time I finish writing this book, I won't need to drive a truck anymore because it will have sold a million copies and helped people live better lives through Jesus Christ our Lord. Then I can get back to playing golf, going fishing, going to church, and praising God. I still want to do all those things—I just hope to be able to do even more of them.

Tiger Woods played in the tournament this week. He had to quit because he played so badly behind, and I know that is not how he wants to play. My point is that everything we do in life has to keep God first, and whatever we do, because it could be taken away from us overnight, and you need Jesus in your life twenty-four hours a day, for all the things that could go wrong in this life. And do not forget life after death, which we call eternal life, that is where we will live forever, and I want to be right with God, so wherever I die, I do not have to worry about going to hell. As I mentioned at the beginning of the book, my brother Calvin was God bless his soul, we just passed on to the game of God.

Now that I have been playing golf for over 30 years, I have all the opportunities that God has created for me. It's a fun game, and it's a game that no one seems to be able to master or take over. It's something that you can learn about Golf and about yourself, as long as you play golf. I've met a lot of great people over the years. I've been to many places, and I've had the chance to do some amazing things. Now, I look forward to even more great things coming from writing this book—

especially the chance to help people understand that life isn't as hard as it seems when you have the right perspective and keep God first in your life.

I also want to share in this book that I love to crappie fish. I usually catch about 12 to 14 inches, but today I caught a crappie almost 16 inches and nearly 2 pounds in the state of Illinois.

Today is 5/22/2022, and I caught a crappie. I love crappie fishing. My wife loves crappie fishing, and I love to play golf. Hopefully, after I finish writing this book, I'll be able to enjoy more of both. I never imagined I'd have to go back to work to support myself and my wife—but I'm thankful I'm able to work and provide for us with a good job. That's why it's so important to always keep your hand in God's hand, because we don't know what life will bring—things we can't handle on our own. We always need the help of our Heavenly Father to get through this life and into the next. If you're reading this book and feel like there's no hope or no one hears your prayers, I want you to know—you're just right for God, especially at your lowest point.

Like I said earlier in the book, I was a drug addicted alcoholic. I felt very helpless and at my lowest, God came to me. He rose me from the ashes.

Today, it's been 40 years since I gained control of my life, and I thank him so much for loving me so much—dying on that cross that I'm able to sit here today and enjoy writing this book and sharing this with you. I really hope someone out there will find help when they feel there is nowhere else to turn.

Today, a young man went into a school and shot over 24 kids, killing them. It was even more, almost 30 or 40 children all died today. This is the kind of world we live in now, and we desperately need prayer. We need to pray and never stop praying because, like I said earlier, this world is not our home.

It's strange to me that we all live in different places and come from different nationalities, but we are all people, and the blood of Jesus Christ flows in us. Someone with a living soul and blood in their body—

and it's that precious blood that makes us all the same in God's eyes. Our spirit, our life—all come from that blood. I thank God that even though we are different people with different backgrounds, we are still one in Him.

I think we need to ask ourselves: What do we want in this life? Who do we want to become? Who do we want to help, and how can we help them?

Thank God for his holy spirit, and thank God for helping me write this book, because I want people to know that without God, I can do nothing, but through Christ Jesus, I can do all things.

I want to give a shout-out to a dear friend of mine, Stephan, who lives in North Carolina, because he makes fun of me for telling him I am on the PGA tour, and I have to go back out on the tour. It just cracks him up when I tell him that I am a tour member and I have the PGA badge; he just does not want to accept the fact that I am the other Woods. I would like to thank Steven Hulka once again for letting me get out on the PGA tour. Without Steven Hulka, this book would not be possible.

My triple bypass surgery happened during the COVID-19 pandemic. I first felt this strange little tingle in my chest and thought maybe I had COVID. I let it go for about a week, but when it got worse, I decided to go to the hospital to get checked out.

At the emergency room, they ran tests, and when the results came back, the doctor told me, "Mr. Woods, you're not going anywhere today." They discovered that I had thirty-five arteries blocked in my heart, and they needed to perform emergency surgery right away. I called my wife and everyone to let them know they wanted to do open-heart surgery on me.

I am going to tell you know they gave me something in that hospital I have never had before in my life, because I had an out-of-body experience. I felt like I was getting some sleep in the hospital, but I was only getting about an hour or two of sleep per night while I was in the hospital. They took me to the operating room and cut my chest wide open, and brought me back, and I don't remember when they cut on me.

I don't remember feeling the knife touch me, and I don't remember anything; that's how strong the drug was that they gave me. All I remember is waking up and feeling kind of crazy in my mind. So after about a week in the hospital after being cut on and all the different drugs pumped into me, they sent me home, and I was so happy to go home. So, my first night at home, I took some medication that they gave me, and right before bed, I took this little bitty pill, which was what it was, but it took me to a new place that I have never been before.

So, my wife went upstairs and got into bed, and I fell asleep in the recliner chair. As I am sleeping in the recliner chair, I come up out of my body in a recliner chair, and I am behind prison bars. I am shaking the prison bars, crying out, and I am hollering: Let me out of here! What is going on. There is nobody in the prison saying anything to me, and it is very damn silent in the prison. As I think the boys and I keep calling where am I God help me I thought I was your child look what is going on I'm taking the boys out here and noise it sounds like something is shutting down and as it's just down it goes *doo doo doo doo* and the third do it gets completely blocked in front of me or I cannot even see my hands I just start screaming real loud and then I wake up.

I woke up and looked around to make sure I was still in the same room. For a moment, I felt like I had left my body and gone somewhere else. I touched myself just to be sure—it really felt like an out-of-body experience, which it was. I got up to use the bathroom, and when I came back, I sat there for about five minutes before falling asleep again. I went back into the same dream, and I repeated that cycle three times. After the third time I woke up, I just started screaming as loud as I could and told my wife Come on, let's go, we've got to go to the doctor right now.

So, we get up and we go to the hospital, and they take me in at the hospital, and I tell him what happened right away, and they looked at all the medications. I remember hearing one of the nurses say Yeah, that's the one that did it right here and something that they gave me wasn't right, and it gave me a stroke.

Are You In Or You Out

Up until that point, I hadn't had any real rest. So, they gave me some kind of pill, and I finally fell asleep in the hospital. I only slept for four hours, but it was solid sleep—felt like I had been out for two days because I was so exhausted. When I woke up, they told me it had only been four hours.

As I lay there in that hospital bed, still feeling the effects of the medication, I could hear demons laughing and giggling around me. I told them firmly, "Get out of my room."

While I was at the hospital, I called everyone I could to tell them about what I experienced—the out-of-body experience. I guess most people thought I was crazy. But I kept talking to each person, including my pastor and some close friends. At the end of every conversation, I'd ask them, "Are you in, or are you out?"

About 30 days later, a movie came out that featured a scene where a woman stands up and says those exact words—"Are you in, or are you out?" It blew a lot of people's minds because I had been preaching that very phrase 30 days before the movie ever came out.

When I saw that movie and heard her say those exact words, I knew it was the same message God had given me—the call to go out and share my testimony, asking people, "Are you in, or are you out?" He never told me to ask about denominations or when someone was born again. God wants everyone on this earth to understand one thing: whether they are in or out when it comes to Christ.

That message stirred something powerful in my spirit. I will keep preaching it, teaching it, and asking everyone this question as I move forward in life because I know God gave it to me. He told me it would ignite a fire in people's souls, making them wonder—are they in, or are they out? I'm committed to being obedient to the Holy Spirit.

It's amazing how God gives you a task and confirms it deep within your spirit—even when it doesn't make sense to those around you.

People might think you're crazy, but when God sends you in a positive direction, you just know it's Him.

I'm so thankful that at this point in my life, God is using me in ways I never imagined. It might sound crazy, but if you read the Bible, you'll see that God often calls His prophets to do things that seem strange or unbelievable. A lot of times when God asks you to do something it does not make sense to the human race but is a good sign that is coming from God when he asks you to do something that just sounds so weird and crazy that you have to wonder yourself what am I doing but I thank God for his holy spirit. So, as I write this book, I will be preaching: *"Are you in or out?"* Exactly how God told me to ask people if they believe in him.

After having a stroke, I had a sixth sense or something. As I write this book, my wife Bertha and I have fallen on some hard times after my heart attack and stroke. Even though things seem a little rough right now, I cannot complain. God has been so good to me and my wife over these 44 years, I dare not complain. I have total faith in God that he will not put more on us than we can bear, and I know that we will have a nice place to live. I thank God that he gives us another day and a chance to do these things. It is one thing to say that we believe in God, but when times get rough, this is when you really need God to come into your life and give you peace that passes all understanding.

After I recovered from my health issues in 2023, I began driving a tractor-trailer for Schnuck Markets, Inc. I thank God for this new chance and the opportunity to write this book, to let you know that God is real in my life—and He can be real in yours too. What I mean is that there are things in life that can't be explained any other way but God's hand at work, not our own.

I just pray that everyone who reads this book understands that I could not have put my life together the way God intended it. I could not have landed a job on the PGA Tour as the caddies' chaplain with the last name Woods during the height of Tiger Woods' dominance on tour. I believe that this was a gift from God, and I know that God wanted me to be there. I also believe that this book will have a significant impact on some people.

I put in my spirit for all that read this book called *"The Other Woods"* that will never pick up a Bible. I hope my personal testimony that I share with you now will be enough for you to believe that God is real, because he has kept me without drugs or alcohol for over 44 years. So, I would encourage anyone to turn their life over to Christ; He can save you. I'm here today to let you know that Jesus is the answer, and you wonder how I know that? It's because he's real in my life, and he can be real in your life. The certain things that go on in my life and in everybody's life you can only give God the credit for, such as writing this book and the things I've been through, it's all been done through God.

I want everyone to know that when God told me to write this book, He made it clear that some of the people who read it may never pick up a Bible. So, I pray that if you are one of those people—reading these words and hearing about Jesus Christ for the first time—you'll come to understand that He was crucified and died on the cross for the sins of the entire world.

You might ask me, "How do you know Jesus died for the sins of the whole world?" I know because I've experienced the power of His love and forgiveness in my own life. The peace, the transformation, and the strength I've received could only come from Him. And what He's done for me, He can also do for you.

It has been 44 years since I have smoked a joint or drank any alcohol and done anything that would make me high. I understand that it is the power of God that has helped me to stay sober and clean for 44 years. I may have lasted 30 days, but not 44 years, and it is a testimony within myself of what God can do. Not only that, there have been so many things that have happened in my life (my wife, my marriage, my job on the PGA tour), all the things that God has given me have kept me and instead of keeping me is the reason I know that God just becomes ruler and realer in my life. and God said he is no respective person that if you trust in Jesus and believe that he died on the cross the guy will come in and he will understand that God is real in your life because there's certain things in our lives as we go through life that only God can handle.

As I write this book, God let me know my testimony in this book may be the only Bible that somebody reads. I know it is hard for people to believe in God when they have never experienced God or even recognize God or who God is. But once we go through life's experiences and understand that some things we encounter, only God can help us with, then we start realizing that God is real. I know that God opened the doors for me to be the caddies' chaplain on the PGA Tour, with the last name Woods, because I have received so many great blessings from being out on tour.

I would like for you to read to me Romans 10th chapter starting at the 8th verse through the 10th verse and believe God's word. The fact that I am writing this book is a witness to God of how good God is. I don't really care if I make a dime off this book, but if I can touch a soul, I have someone to believe that God is real; that is my purpose for writing this book. Tiger Woods has a net worth of a billion dollars or more, and people often overlook the fact that this world is not our home. Through Christ Jesus, we have more than enough, as He supplies all our needs according to His riches. I know that God will continue to provide for our needs according to His riches.

If you are reading this book and you are struggling with life and things seem hard to you, I want you to know that God makes life very simple for us. All you have to do is just talk to God just like He is your Heavenly Father in plain language and just ask Him to do for you what you can't do for yourself. He can help you with whatever you're feeling, and I guarantee you that if you're sincere, God will help you with whatever problems you have right now. That is what faith is all about— when God answers your prayers and you see that God is real in your own personal life, because we must have personal contact with God. We can't get in on our parents' faith, we can't get in on our grandparents' faith—we must have a personal relationship with God. That's why when people try to talk to you and try to tell you things that are not true, you must experience God and His goodness for yourself; you can't go by what somebody else says.

I am writing this book because I know that in my life, I've had so many things happen, and God has blessed me in so many ways, and I just need to share it with you all before I leave this earth. Tiger Woods was in a very bad car accident and almost lost his life in 2021. He walked away from the car accident, and he is coming back playing some golf, but it just goes to show you, no matter how much money we have, how much pain we have, we all must die and leave here. So, at some point we must have a relationship with God because we will meet God when we die. One thing I love about Tiger Woods is that he never gives up; he always pushes forward. When it looked like the accident would have stopped him from ever playing golf again, he pushed through all the pain and did everything he needed to do to get back on tour. It lets me know that if you put your mind to it, you can do anything. I am glad Tiger Woods recovered from his accident. It is times like these when we really find out if God is real or not.

www.ingramcontent.com/pod-product-compliance
Lightning Source LLC
Chambersburg PA
CBHW050728010526
44107CB00009B/779